PIONEERS IN SCIENCE

BIOLOGY

PETER LAFFERTY

HEINEMANN

First published in 1992 by
Heinemann Children's Reference,
a division of Heinemann Educational Books Ltd,
Halley Court, Jordan Hill, Oxford OX2 8EJ

OXFORD LONDON EDINBURGH
MADRID PARIS ATHENS BOLOGNA
MELBOURNE SYDNEY AUKLAND SINGAPORE TOKYO
IBADAN NAIROBI GABORONE HARARE
PORTSMOUTH (NH)

Project manager Myra Murby
Editor Mary Melling
Designer Jerry Burman
Picture researchers Catherine Blackie, Suzanne Williams

Printed in Hong Kong

British Library Cataloguing in Publication Data

Lafferty, Peter
Biology. – (Pioneers in science)
1. Biology, history
I. Title II. Series
574.0922

ISBN 0-431-00795-0

Photographic acknowledgements

t=top b=bottom r=right l=left c=centre

The Bridgeman Art Library/Vatican, Rome 7; Bridgeman Art Library 15t; Bridgeman Art Library/Royal College of Surgeons, London 28; C. M. Dixon 6b; E. T. Archive 14; Frank Spooner Pictures 25r; Genus 17t; Michael Holford 4; The Hulton Picture Company 5t, 6t, 8, 21t, 30b, 32; The Hutchison Library/Nancy Durrell-McKenna 30t; Mary Evans Picture Library 9l & r, 12, 16, 18, 23t, & b, 24, 29r; Oxford Scientific Films/Scott Camazine 11t; Oxford Scientific Films/Richard Packwood 15bl; Oxford Scientific Films/Okapia 15br; Oxford Scientific films/Fredrik Ehrenstrom 19bl; Oxford Scientific Films/Maryn Chillmaid 19br; Oxford Scientific Films/London Scientific films 27t; Oxford Scientific films/G. I. Bernard 27cl, cr & b; Oxford Scientific Films/D. R. Specker 37t; Oxford Scientific films/Alastair Shay 37b; Oxford University Museum 22; Radio Times 38l; Ann Ronan Picture Library 11b, 13tl & br, 26; Science Photo Library/Lawrence Nightingale 5b; Science Photo Library/Jeremy Burgess 10t, 33t; Science Photo Library/Marcos Loez 17b; Science Photo Library/David Giffard 20; Science Photo Library/David Scharf 251; Science Photo Library/John Reader 29l, 34t & b, 35; Science Photo Library/CNRI 40; Science Photo Library/Dr L. Card 41l; Science Photo Library/Damien Schouvaert 41r; Science Photo Library/Chemical Design 43t; Science Photo Library/Peter Menzel 43b; Supplied by Syndication International © Roger Hyde 31; Sally Anne Thompson 33bl & br; Taurus Graphics 39b; Weidenfeld & Nicolson Archives/Photo A. C. Barrington-Brown 42

Cover: Mary Evans Picture Library l; E. T. Archive c; The Bettmann Archive r; H. C. Baillie b.
Cover pictures show: George Cuvier l; Carl von Linné (Linnaeus) c; Thomas Morgan r; Painted Lady butterfly b.

Note to the reader
In this book there are some words in the text that are printed in bold type. This shows that the word is listed in the glossary on page 46. The glossary gives a brief explanation of words that may be new to you.

Contents

Introduction

Where do we come from? What makes plants grow? Why do birds fly? These are just some of the questions people have always asked about the world around them. The study of living things is called **biology** and someone who studies living things is called a **biologist**.

Biology is probably the oldest **science**. Long ago, when people lived by hunting animals and gathering fruits and plants to eat, they needed to know how the animals lived so that they could catch them. They also needed to know which plants were safe to eat. So they had to study animals and plants. Today, the study of animals is called **zoology** and the study of plants is called **botany**. Zoology and botany are both kinds of biology.

Making discoveries

Biologists make discoveries like other scientists by looking carefully at what they are studying and doing **experiments**. An experiment is a test done to discover something new, or to discover if an idea is correct. Some experiments make measurements. For instance, a biologist might measure how much a plant grows in a day. Other experiments see how plants and animals change if their surroundings change. If a biologist thinks that plants need warmth in order to grow well, they might put a plant in a heated room to see if the heat makes it grow faster. The experiment would find out if this idea is correct. An idea that tries to explain why something happens is called a **theory**.

Cave painting from Altimira, northern Spain. Some cave paintings found in France and Spain are over 30,000 years old. Most, like this one of a bison, are very realistic. The artist must have studied the animals very carefully, like a scientist. This was the beginning of zoology, the scientific study of animals.

A herb garden, 1533. Plants have been used as herbs in cooking, and as medicines, since early times. Gardeners had to study useful plants carefully to learn which conditions suited them. This was the beginning of botany, the scientific study of plants.

Some biologists have invented useful instruments to carry out their experiments. A magnifying glass helps them see small animals and plants more clearly and a much more powerful instrument, called the **microscope**, is used to look at very small animals and plants. The invention of the microscope was one of the most important developments in biology. It has helped many biologists make discoveries that have changed the way we think about the world.

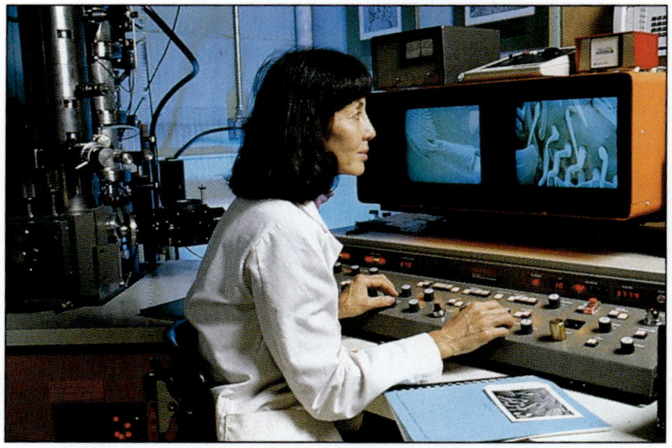

A modern biologist at work. This scientist is seated at the controls of an electron microscope, one main tool of the biologist today. The instrument can magnify, or enlarge, over a million times. This is powerful enough to see the smallest living things. On the screen is an enlarged picture of an insect leg.

Strange ideas

This book tells the story of many of these famous biologists, the experiments they did and what they discovered. People often had strange ideas about the natural world before these biologists made their discoveries. For instance, it was once thought that old bits of dirty cloth could change into mice!

It was also believed that some plants screamed when they were pulled out of the ground. A simple experiment would have shown this was wrong. All that anyone had to do was to pull the plant out of the earth and listen for a scream. But until about 400 years ago, people did not know that experiments like this were the best way to discover the truth.

The beginning of science

Scientific study began about 2000 years ago in Greece. At that time, many new ideas were being discussed. A famous teacher called Aristotle began to use experiments and scientific methods to study animals. Aristotle was born in a small town on the coast of Greece over 2000 years ago. When he was 17, he went to Athens to study. This city had a school called the Academy run by a brilliant teacher called Plato. Aristotle was very clever and he spent 20 years studying with Plato, learning all he could.

When Plato died in 347BC, Aristotle went to live on the island of Lesbos near the country now called Turkey. It was there that he became interested in biology. Aristotle studied the animals that he found in the sea around the island. He learned a great deal by talking to fishermen and by cutting up fish, squid and octopus.

Aristotle, the first real scientist, who lived in Greece from 384BC until 322BC. For over 2000 years, most scientific theories were based on his ideas and observations.

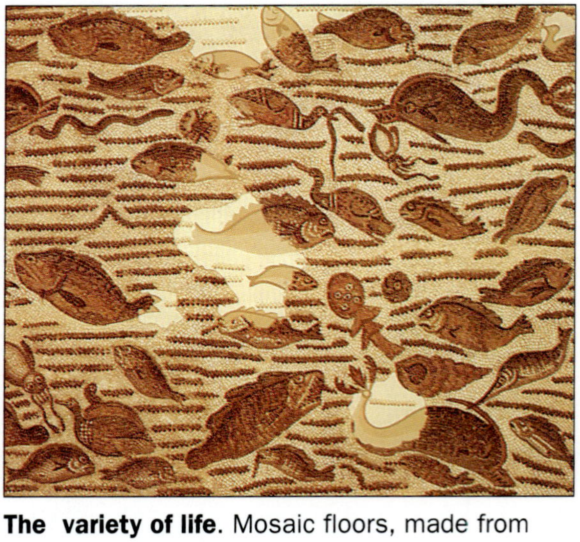

The variety of life. Mosaic floors, made from small chips of coloured stone, were popular in Greek and Roman times. This Roman mosaic floor from Carthage, on the north African coast, shows many different types of fish. Aristotle studied the fish and other animals found in the seas around Greece.

Hatching chickens

Aristotle did not believe anything until he had seen it for himself. He wanted to know how chicks grew inside an egg so he placed 20 eggs under a hen for hatching. Each day he took one egg out. He broke it open and looked inside. He saw that after about three days a tiny speck forms in the sharp end of the egg. After ten days, this tiny speck grows into a small chick. After 20 days, the chick moves inside the egg and makes a chirping sound. The next day, the chick begins to break open the shell. Aristotle was the first person ever to do an experiment like this.

Teacher, writer and scientist

Aristotle was only on Lesbos for three years. Then, King Philip of Macedonia, a part of Greece, asked him to teach his son, Alexander. When Alexander became king, he set out to conquer new lands and he became known as Alexander the Great. During his time as Alexander's tutor, Aristotle began to write a huge book containing all that was known about the living world at the time. In his book, he showed that the Earth was round. He wrote about the stars, the way things move, the winds and the weather and rocks. Finally, he described his discoveries about animals. When he had finished his book he returned to Athens to start his own school, which he called the Lyceum, where he taught his ideas. He also collected books and maps.

Aristotle was one of the most important biologists because he showed how essential it is to look carefully at the things around us and how important it is to do experiments. This is why Aristotle is said to be the first real scientist.

The school at Athens. This painting was painted by the Italian artist Raphael in 1509. It shows Aristotle and Plato walking through the Lyceum, or school, at Athens. They are surrounded by scholars studying or debating. On the left, a geometry diagram is the centre of attention.

Too small to see?

Some living things are so small that they are difficult, or impossible, to see with the naked eye. If you look through a magnifying glass the things you see are enlarged or magnified. A magnifying glass consists of a piece of glass with curved sides called a **lens**. For a long time, this was the only way scientists could examine small objects. In about 1590, a Dutch spectacle maker called Zacharias Janssen discovered how to use two lenses to see extremely small objects. He used one of the lenses to magnify the **image**, or picture, produced by the other lens. This was the first microscope.

Other scientists soon improved the microscope. By about 1612 the Italian scientist, Galileo Galilei, had made one that magnified 50 000 times, making a flea seem as big as a hen. Since then the microscope has been an important tool for biologists because it allows them to study the tiniest organisms, or living things.

Robert Hooke

Robert Hooke was an English scientist who was born in 1635. Hooke made many important discoveries and he was the first person to use a microscope for scientific investigations. Hooke examined insects and plants, using a microscope that he had made himself. When he looked at a piece of cork he discovered that it was made up of small box-shaped parts that he called **cells**. Later scientists, such as Theodor Schwann, showed that all living things are made up of cells. Hooke made beautiful drawings

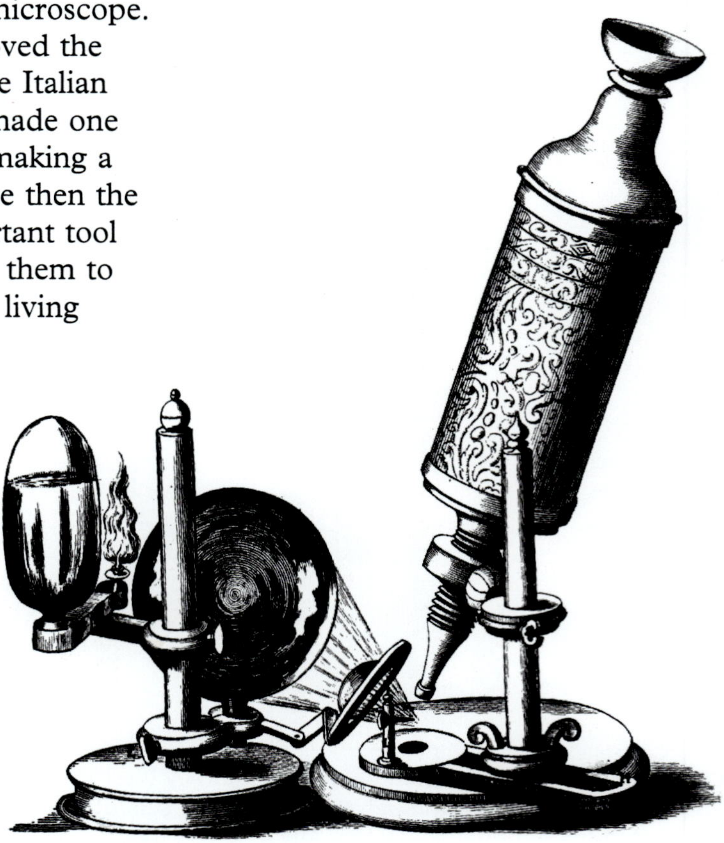

Robert Hooke's microscope. Made in 1665, Robert Hooke's microscope was difficult to use. It needed a bright light, from the frame at the left, which was concentrated by a ball of glass. The microscope was moved up and down to obtain a clear picture.

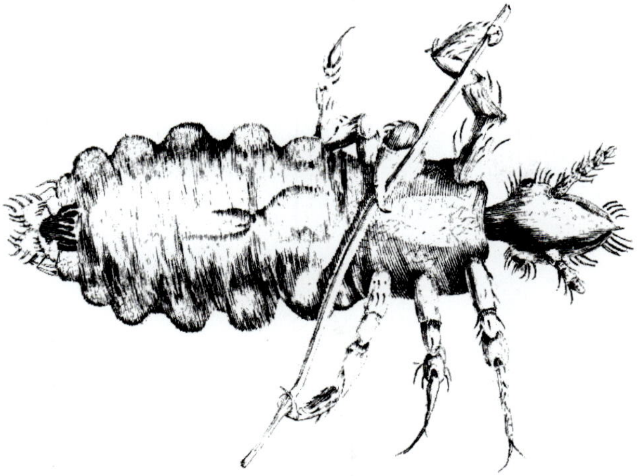

An insect seen through Hooke's microscope. Hooke made excellent drawings of what he saw through his microscope. The picture shows Hooke's very accurate drawing of a louse attached to a hair.

of what he saw through his microscope. These were printed in a book in 1665. Unfortunately, Hooke's microscope was difficult to use. It produced blurred, coloured images that were hard to make out. In the end, Hooke's eyesight was damaged by too much staring into the microscope.

Anton van Leeuwenhoek (1632–1723) who designed and built his own microscopes. Using a single lens, they could magnify up to 200 times and so he could see further into the magnified world than other microscopists. His observations and discoveries revolutionized the science of biology.

Anton van Leeuwenhoek

A Dutchman called Anton van Leeuwenhoek made a different kind of microscope using a single lens. As a boy, he worked in a shop where one of his jobs was to examine cloth using a magnifying glass. Whenever possible he liked to look at other things through his glass.

Van Leeuwenhoek soon made a microscope of his own. He used a single, very fat lens that looked like a small pebble. This worked well and he was able to study insects, such as the aphid and the flea. In 1674 he examined a drop of rain water taken from a barrel near his house. He discovered that it was filled with 'wretched beasties moving about very nimbly'. Although he did not realize it, these 'beasties' were **bacteria**, or germs, that can cause disease. Later scientists, such as Louis Pasteur, showed how to kill bacteria and so prevent disease. By Pasteur's time, however, microscopes using two lenses had been improved and single lens microscopes were no longer used.

Jan Swammerdam

Jan Swammerdam was a Dutch scientist who used the microscope to study small plants and insects. He was born in Amsterdam in 1637, the son of a wealthy merchant. His father's ships sailed all over the world and they brought back many strange and interesting plants and animals, which were stored in a museum. Young Jan helped in the museum, and began studying the exhibits. When he was older, he studied medicine at Leyden University near Amsterdam. It was during his studies that he began using a microscope.

In 1658 he discovered that the blood of frogs contained small red objects that he called **corpuscles**. Later scientists found these same red corpuscles in human blood. Red corpuscles carry life-giving oxygen around the body.

A closer look

While resting in the country after an illness, Swammerdam began to use his microscope to study insects. He carefully cut them open to see how their bodies were made. He cut up and examined bees, wasps, ants, gnats, dragonflies and mayflies, comparing one with another. He drew pictures of the **intestines**, or food tubes, of the bee. He discovered that a bee's eye is made up of many small eyes joined together. Each small eye points in a different direction, and so the insect is able to see in all directions at once. He also discovered how the

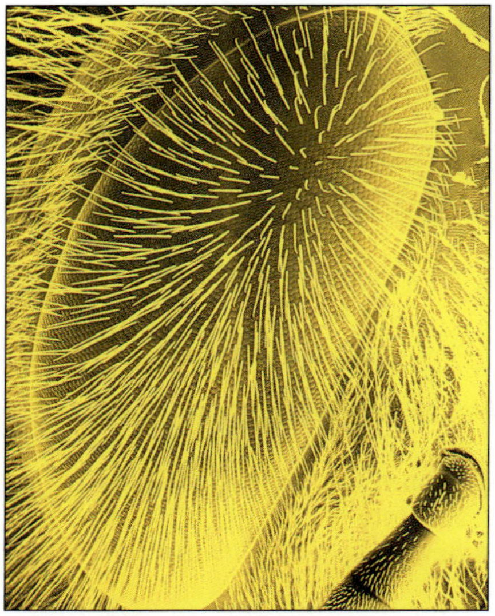

The eye of a honeybee. Magnified about 50 times, the eye has long bristles. These hide the many small eyes which are joined together. A single, tiny pollen grain is caught in the bristles on the edge of the eye, the top right. One of the bee's antennae is seen at the bottom right.

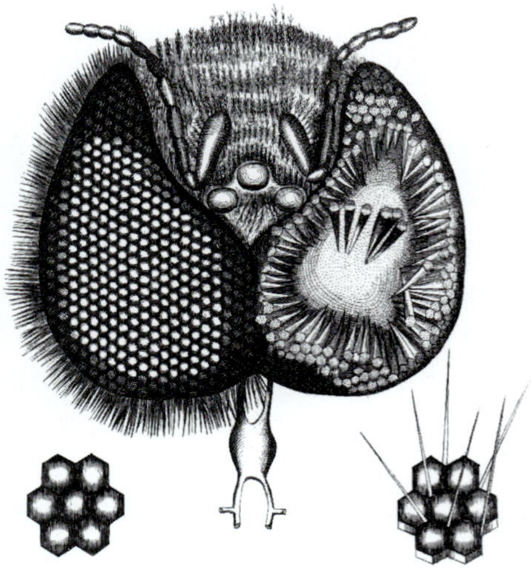

Swammerdam's drawing of a bee's eye. Dutch scientist Jan Swammerdam (1637–1680) was the first to see that a bee's eye was made up of many separate hexagonal eyes. This lets the bee see in all directions at once. His drawing also shows the fine hairs that cover the eyes.

A queen honeybee surrounded by some workers. The queen lays eggs in the empty cells. Jan Swammerdam studied the way the queen produced eggs.

Jan Swammerdam being followed by a swarm of bees because he has taken their queen.

bee's sting works and he studied how the queen bee produces eggs.

Although he became almost blind by working in the bright summer sunlight, he carried on, studying the way insects change during their lives. Tadpoles also interested him, so he carefully observed how they grew into frogs. When examining a frog, he made a discovery about the nerves, the long thread-like organs that carry messages between the brain and other parts of the body. Most people at the time thought that nerves were hollow tubes containing a liquid. They believed that this liquid flowed into the muscles to make them swell up. However, using his microscope, Swammerdam saw that nerves were not hollow and there was no liquid inside them.

The Bible of Nature

Swammerdam died in 1680 but his discoveries live on. Forty years after his death, a book was printed showing all his drawings of insects and other living things. The book was called *The Bible of Nature* and it is still used by many naturalists today. It is the best collection of drawings of insects ever made using a microscope. Swammerdam's friend, Hermann Boerhaave, said, 'From the beginning of nature study to our own time, nobody has been able to equal his work.'

How plants drink

One of the greatest scientific discoveries was finding out how blood flows through the body. In 1682 an English doctor called William Harvey suggested that blood flowed around the body in a circular path. Harvey's theory was that blood left the heart through tubes called the **arteries** and then returned to the heart by travelling through the **veins**. This circular flow was called the **circulation** of the blood.

Stephen Hales was the vicar of Teddington near London. He was also interested in science and he wanted to prove that Harvey was right. In order to do this he had to cut open animals such as horses, dogs and frogs to see how the blood vessels were arranged. Many people objected to his gruesome experiments, but they were necessary to find the truth. Hales showed that Harvey's theory was right.

Do plants have circulation?

Then Hales wondered about plants. Did the liquid, called **sap**, inside plants travel in a circle from the roots to the leaves and back again? In 1716 Hales did a simple experiment. He cut a large branch from an apple tree. A tube containing water was joined to the branch at the bottom. Then he cut the bark a little way above the tube. After a while, Hales saw the water in the tube disappear. It was travelling up the branch towards the leaves. But no water

Stephen Hales (1677–1761) studied how blood flowed through the bodies of animals. To do this, he had to cut up the bodies of many dead animals. Many people were upset, thinking his experiments were too cruel.

appeared at the cut in the bark, coming down from the leaves. This showed that water travelled up to the leaves. Hales thought that the water went from the leaves out into the air.

Hales did another simple experiment to prove that the leaves gave out water. He put a small tree branch inside a closed glass bottle. After a while, the inside of the glass was covered with small droplets of water. These droplets had been given off by the leaves.

A busy vicar

Hales was not only a vicar and a scientist. He helped to govern the American colony of Georgia and the British government asked him to help improve the living conditions on naval

◀ **Stephen Hales's discoveries were printed in a book, *Vegetable Staticks*, in 1725**. This page illustrates an experiment to measure the force with which sap rises.

▼ **Hales's experiment on the circulation of sap, c 1727**. A tube of water was fixed to the end of an apple branch. The bark was cut away above the join. The lower edge of the cut bark became moist but the upper edge stayed dry. This showed that water rose up the stem but that none came down from the leaves.

ships. He became interested in the best way of getting fresh air to the sailors below decks and he invented a device for improving the flow of air, which the Royal Navy used in its ships. He died in 1761, still the vicar of Teddington, but also a well-known scientist. His discovery that plants give off water has helped other scientists to study how much water plants need to grow and how evaporation from their leaves affects the climate.

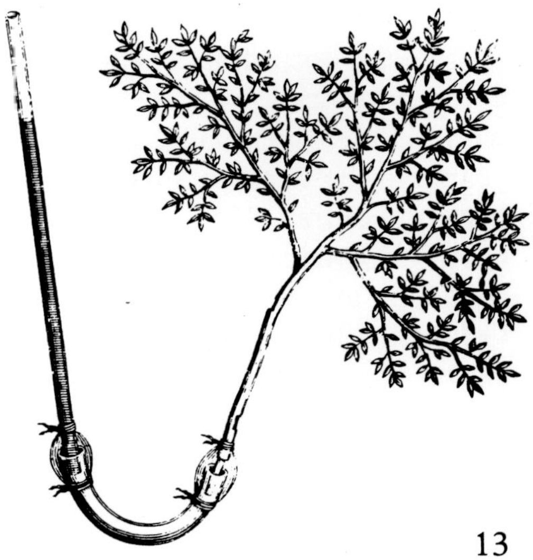

Naming animals and plants

Every language has its own name for animals and plants. A bear is called *orso* in Italian, and *ours* in French. Sometimes the same name is used for different animals in different parts of the world. People used to get very confused and mistakes were often made about which plant or animal was being described. To avoid confusion, biologists now use Latin, the language of the Romans, to name plants and animals. In this way they can be sure what plant or animal they are talking about. The man who first decided to give Latin names to plants and animals was Carl von Linné. He even changed his own name into Latin, Carolus Linnaeus.

Carl von Linné (Linneaus) (1707–78) showed how to give names to plants and animals in a systematic way. A much-loved teacher, he travelled widely to collect specimens of plants and animals. Here he is shown during a trip to Lapland in 1732.

The little botanist

Linnaeus was born in 1707 in a small village called Rashult, in Sweden. He was the son of the village clergyman. He was always interested in plants and his nickname was 'the little botanist', because he was always collecting plants. He was a poor pupil at school, and could not decide what he wanted to do with his life. Eventually, when he was 23 years old, he became a teacher of botany. He travelled in Lapland, in the north of Sweden, and other countries, collecting and studying plants. Gradually, he became famous and his classes were very popular. In 1741, he became professor of botany and medicine at Uppsala University in Sweden. He persuaded his pupils to travel widely to collect plants and in this way he built up a large collection of plants and insects.

Dividing plants into groups

Linnaeus began to see that some plants were similar, and seemed to belong together. In 1758 he showed how to divide plants into groups. Each group contained similar plants. Grouping similar things together in this way is called **classifying**. It is an essential part of studying living things. After he had put the plants into groups, Linnaeus gave each plant a two-part Latin name.

Naming flowers systematically. This illustration from a book published in 1736 explains how Linneaus named different types of flowers.

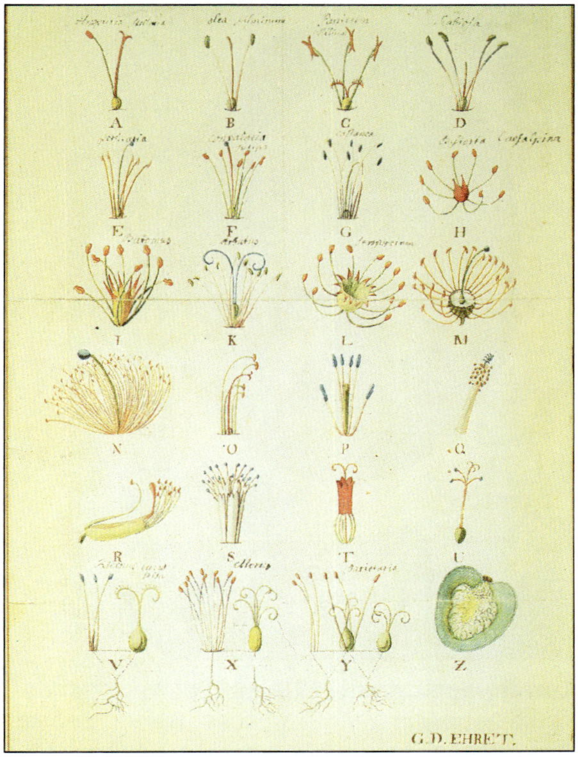

The first part of the name was called the **genus**. The second part of the name was called the **species**. The two names together showed exactly what a plant was. For instance, Linnaeus gave all the flowers called primroses a genus name of *primula*. One kind of primrose with purple flowers he called the species *versus*. So the full name of the purple primrose is *primula versus*. In this way, Linnaeus was able to classify and name thousands of plants.

In 1735 Linnaeus wrote a book explaining his ideas called *Systema Naturae*. Although the book was only 12 pages long, it marked the beginning of modern botany. His method of giving a two-part name to plants is also used to name animals and is still used today by all biologists.

▲ **Two-part names.** Linneaus gave two-part names to plants and animals. The first name, called the *genus,* indicated the kind of plant or animal being named. The second name, called the *species*, indicated the particular type of plant or animal. For example, the African elephant (**left**) and the Indian elephant (**right**) are both elephants so they both have the same first name, or genus, *Elephans*, but a different second name to describe the species. The scientific name of the African elephant is *Elephans africanus*. The Indian elephant is called *Elephans indicus*.

How life begins

It is hard to believe that until a few hundred years ago no one really knew how life started. People used to have some very strange ideas about the way animals come to life. Many years ago, a monk wrote that if some cheese and old rags were put together, mice would be born from them. Some people thought that maggots appeared in rotting meat spontaneously, or without any cause. This was called the 'spontaneous generation' of life.

The person who showed these ideas were wrong was an Italian priest called Lazzaro Spallanzani. Spallanzani was born in Italy in 1729. He studied law but became interested in science. Then he became a priest and taught biology in the Italian city of Pavia.

Lazzaro Spallanzani (1729–99) proved that life could not begin without a cause. Before, people had strange ideas about how animals came to life. Scientists continued to argue even after Spallanzani's experiments but eventually, French scientist Louis Pasteur showed Spallanzani was right.

An experiment with broth

In one of his experiments, Spallanzani heated a vegetable broth and then put it in an air-tight bottle. He found that the broth did not go bad when it was left like this, even for quite a long time. The bacteria that normally cause broth to go bad did not appear spontaneously in the bottle. Spallanzani realized that the bacteria must usually come from the air and because the bottle was air-tight, they could not get into the broth.

Many people did not believe this. They thought that bacteria appeared spontaneously in the broth. However, in 1857, Spallanzani's experiments were repeated by the famous French scientist, Louis Pasteur. He showed that Spallanzani was right. The bacteria that cause food to go bad are floating in the air. To stop food from going bad, either the bacteria must be stopped from getting into the food, or any bacteria in the food must be killed. This is why today milk is heated before it is put into bottles. Any bacteria in the milk are killed by the heat and this keeps the milk from going bad quickly. This process is called **pasteurization**, after Louis Pasteur.

▲ **Better breeding of animals**. Spallanzani was the first person to perform artificial insemination. He put sperm from a male dog into a female dog to produce puppies. Today, farmers use the same method to breed better animals, such as the bull shown in the picture which in turn has fathered thousands of calves.

Having babies

In Pavia, Spallanzani studied the way blood flows, or circulates, in the body, and the way animals breathe. His most important work, however, was to find out how life begins. He discovered that in order for **female** animals to have babies, **sperm**, a substance made by a **male** animal, has to enter the female's body. Spallanzani proved this by using sperm from a male dog to make a female dog have puppies. Today, farmers do the same thing to make their cows have calves. Sperm is taken from a bull and put into a cow. This process is called **artificial insemination**. Using artificial insemination, farmers can make sure that their animals will produce young at the best time. Spallanzani's discovery was a vital first step in the understanding of how animals reproduce.

A modern plant for pasteurizing milk. This process kills all the bacteria or germs in the milk. Spallanzani and Louis Pasteur, a French scientist, showed that foods could not go bad if they did not contain live bacteria.

Jean Lamarck

Jean Lamarck was a famous French scientist who invented the word 'biology' as the name for the study of living things. He was born in 1744. Lamarck was most famous for his ideas on how animals changed over periods of time. Although some of his ideas were eventually proved wrong by later biologists, many of his other ideas are still used today.

Jean Lamark (1744–1829) a French naturalist, invented the word 'biology' to describe the study of living things. He suggested that living things change, or evolve, over long periods of time. This is true, but the changes do not occur in the way Lamark thought. Later scientists, such as Charles Darwin, found how evolution really works.

The royal gardener

Lamarck studied at a college in Amiens in northern France. Later, he joined the army, but he had to leave because of an injury. He then went to Paris to study medicine, and it was there that he became interested in botany, the study of plants. In 1778 he wrote a book on French flowers. This was the first time French flowers had been studied carefully. The book did not earn him any money, so he got a job as the keeper of the King's garden. This did not pay well either but it allowed him to read and to study. In 1793 he became professor of zoology in Paris.

In the years that followed, Lamarck realized something that no one had previously noticed. He discovered that animals could be divided into two groups. Some animals, which he called **vertebrates**, had backbones. Others, which he called **invertebrates**, had no backbones. Vertebrates included such animals as dogs, cats, birds, snakes, fish and human beings. Invertebrates included animals like worms, starfish, and jellyfish. This important way of grouping, or classifying, animals is still used today.

Why the giraffe has a long neck

During his work, Lamarck became convinced that animals could gradually change, or **evolve**, so that over long periods of time they became better suited to their surroundings. He thought they picked up new habits or were changed by their surroundings. He also thought that if an animal changed, its babies would also be changed in the same way. For example, if a woman became tanned because of living in a hot

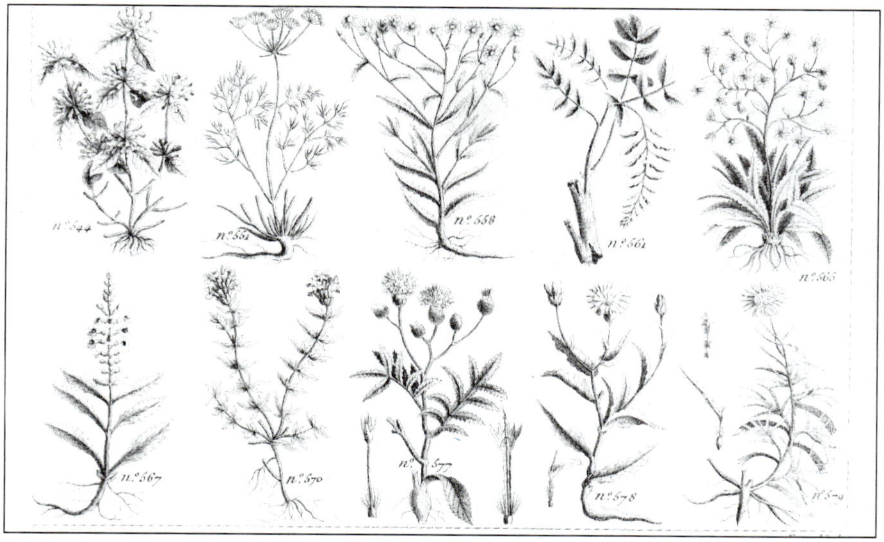

French flowers studied by Lamark. This illustration is from the first botanical study of French flowers written by Lamark in 1788. Lamark was the first botanist to make such a careful study of flowers.

climate, her babies would be dark-skinned. Another example is the giraffe. Lamarck thought that the giraffe had a long neck because it had stretched to reach to the tops of trees to get food. When baby giraffes were born, they too would have long necks.

Lamarck believed that whole populations of animals would gradually change or evolve. He thought that this was why there were so many different types of animals in the world and that the different animals had evolved to suit their surroundings. Fifty years later, other scientists, like Charles Darwin, proved that animals do evolve, as Lamarck suspected. Although they do not change in the quite the way Lamarck thought, it was Lamarck's ideas that helped later scientists discover how living creatures evolve.

Classifying animals. Jean Lamark, the greatest zoologist of his time, discovered that animals could be divided into two groups: vertebrates (animals with backbones), and invertebrates (animals without backbones). The jellyfish on the left is an invertebrate, the dog on the right is a vertebrate.

Food processing

What happens to food when you swallow it? After the food enters the stomach, it is **digested**. This means it is softened and dissolved so that your body can soak up the goodness in the food. Many years ago most people thought this process was a kind of cooking and that the heat of the stomach digested the food. About three hundred years ago, a Flemish doctor called Jan van Helmont thought differently. He said that fish digest their food, but they are cold-blooded and have no heat in their bodies. He thought the answer was that there were **acid** juices in the stomach, which dissolved the food. However, he could not be sure. It was not until two hundred years later that an American doctor called William Beaumont proved that he was correct.

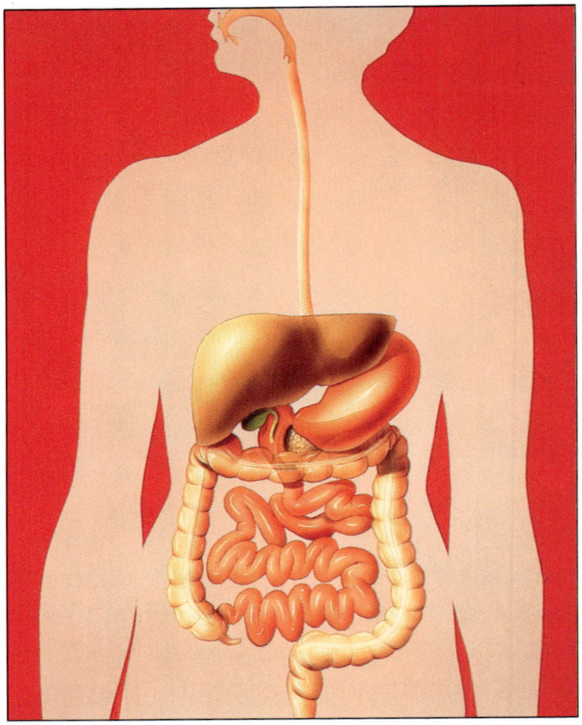

Our digestive system is a long tube that starts at the mouth. The stomach, top right, under the liver is a muscular bag that acts like a cement mixer. It churns up food and starts digesting and then absorbing it. The large and small intestines are seen below the stomach and liver.

A brave soldier

William Beaumont was born in 1785 in Connecticut, on the east coast of the United States. He left home when he was 21 years old to seek adventure, taking with him a horse, a knife, a barrel of cider and $100. When his money and cider were gone, he took a job as a teacher in New York. He borrowed books on medicine and eventually became a doctor. In 1812, when the United States was at war with Britain, he joined the army.

In 1822 a soldier named Alexis St Martin was wounded when a musket was fired accidentally. He was brought to William Beaumont for help. There were several wounds, including a hole in the front of his body, near his stomach. Beaumont saw that the food the soldier had eaten at breakfast was coming out of this hole. With Beaumont's help Alexis St Martin gradually recovered.

A strong stomach

However, the hole in St Martin's stomach did not close up completely and Beaumont realized that he could use it to

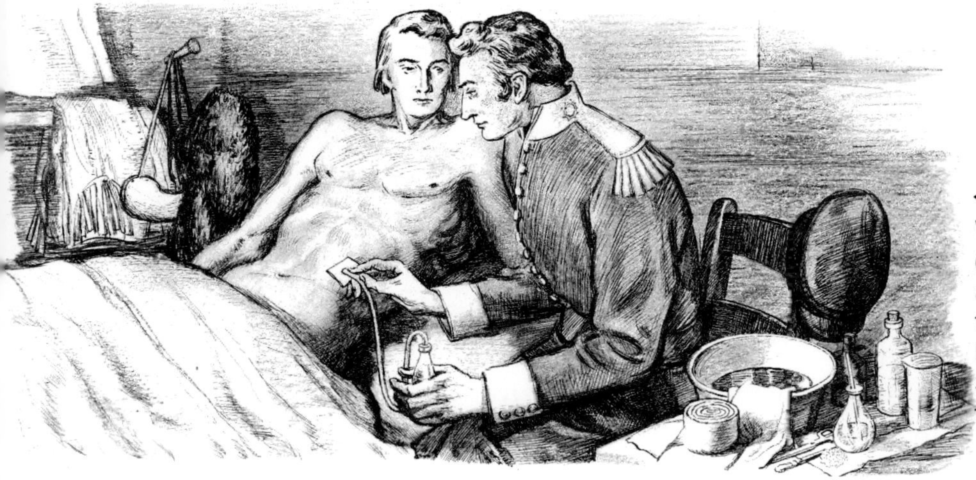

◀ American doctor William Beaumont (1785–1853) took advantage of a hole in the stomach of a young French Canadian, Alexis St Martin, to study how food is digested.

study how St Martin's stomach worked. He began to do experiments. He looked into the hole to see how quickly food was digested. He measured the temperature inside the stomach. He even took juices out of the stomach to see if they would dissolve food outside the body.

William Beaumont was able to prove that the acids and other chemicals in the stomach soften and dissolve food even when the stomach juices are outside the stomach. He also studied how long it took to dissolve different foods. It took about five hours to dissolve a piece of fish, and one hour to dissolve boiled rice.

Luckily, St Martin was a strong young man. He survived all the poking and pulling of food through the hole. He even remained good friends with Beaumont! Beaumont's discoveries about digestion mean that we know how long to wait after a meal before going swimming, what foods will quickly give us energy and what foods may cause problems.

ARTICLES OF DIET.	Mean Time of Chymification.			
	In Stomach.		In Vials.	
	Preparation.	H. M.	Preparation.	H. M.
Rice,	Boiled	1		
Pig's feet, soused,	Boiled	1		
Tripe, soused,	Boiled	1		
Eggs, whipped,	Raw	1 30	Whipped	4
Trout, salmon, fresh,	Boiled	1 30	Boiled	3 30
Trout, salmon, fresh,	Fried	1 30		
Soup, barley,	Boiled	1 30		
Apples, sweet, mellow,	Raw	1 30	Masticated	6 45
Venison steak,	Broiled	1 35		
Brains, animal,	Boiled	1 45	Boiled	4 30
Sago,	Boiled	1 45	Boiled	3 15
Tapioca,	Boiled	2	Boiled	3 20
Barley,	Boiled	2		
Milk,	Boiled	2	Boiled	4 15
Liver, beef's, fresh,	Broiled	2	Cut fine	6 30
Eggs, fresh,	Raw	2	Raw	4 15
Codfish, cured dry,	Boiled	2	Boiled	5
Apples, sour, mellow,	Raw	2	Masticated	8 30
Cabbage, with vinegar,	Raw	2	Shaved	10 15
Milk,	Raw	2 15	Raw	4 45
Eggs, fresh,	Roasted	2 15		
Turkey, wild,	Roasted	2 18		
Turkey, domestic,	Boiled	2 25		
Gelatine,	Boiled	2 30	Boiled	4 45
Turkey, domestic,	Roasted	2 30		
Goose, wild,	Roasted	2 30		
Pig, sucking,	Roasted	2 30		
Lamb, fresh,	Broiled	2 30		
Hash, meat and vegetables,	Warmed	2 30		
Beans, pod,	Boiled	2 30		
Cake, sponge,	Baked	2 30	Broken	6 15
Parsneps,	Boiled	2 30	Mashed	6 45
Potatoes, Irish,	Roasted	2 30		
Potatoes, Irish,	Baked	2 30		

Experiments on digestion. William Beaumont compared the time it took for food to be digested naturally in the stomach with the time taken in a laboratory experiment. The stomach is much more efficient.

Discovering the dinosaurs

Dinosaurs were creatures like lizards that lived millions of years ago, long before people lived on the Earth. There were many different types of dinosaurs. Some were as small as rabbits and some were ten times larger than elephants. Most dinosaurs were peaceful plant eaters but others were fierce, and ate other animals. The dinosaurs died out about 65 million years ago. We know about the dinosaurs because their bones have been preserved in old rocks. The rock-like remains of dead animals and plants are called **fossils**.

In 1770 a surprising discovery was made deep in a mine in Holland. The miners found the jaws of a huge animal preserved in the rocks. The discovery caused a lot of arguments. Eventually a famous French scientist, Georges Cuvier, proved that the jaws came from a gigantic lizard that had died long ago. Fifty years later, more enormous fossil bones were discovered in England by Gideon Mantell.

Mysterious teeth

Gideon Mantell was a country doctor in the small town of Lewes in southern England. His hobby was looking for fossils. In about 1822 Mantell's wife found some fossil teeth by the roadside. Mantell found more of the teeth in a nearby quarry. At first he could not identify the teeth. He showed them to Cuvier in Paris and to William Buckland, a scientist in Oxford, an important university town in England. However, the teeth remained a mystery.

Later Mantell noticed that the teeth were like the teeth of a South American lizard, the iguana. He realized that they

The discovery of Mosasaurus. A huge fossil jaw bone was discovered in a chalk mine in Holland in 1770. The French scientist Georges Cuvier proved that the bones were the remains of an extinct lizard that lived in the sea millions of years earlier.

◀ **A strange dinner party**. Between 1852 and 1854, Richard Owen made many life-sized models of dinosaurs to put in an exhibition. To celebrate completion of this huge task, a dinner party was held inside the body of the model iguanodon. The guests were rather cramped.

▶ **Georges Cuvier (1769–1832)**. He used fossils to prove that giant reptiles had existed long ago. He believed that these animals had been destroyed in floods that covered the Earth.

must come from a huge long-dead lizard that was like the **iguana**. He called it the **iguanodon**. Later he found the fossil remains of other huge lizards and his friend William Buckland also found the remains of a big lizard near Oxford.

Richard Owen's terrible lizards

In 1841 Richard Owen, another British scientist, became interested in these fossils. He saw that the fossils discovered by Mantell and Buckland were very different from any other lizards. He thought they deserved a name of their own, so he called them 'dinosaurs'. This name means 'terrible lizards' in Greek.

By looking at all the different bones discovered, he was able to see what the dinosaurs had looked like and he made life-size models of them. In 1850 these models were shown at an exhibition in London. They created great interest because people had never seen anything like them. Not long after this, dinosaur bones were discovered in the United States. These showed that there were many different kinds of dinosaur. Since then, people have found complete skeletons of dinosaurs and many museums have skeletons and models of dinosaurs on show. It is thanks to the discoveries of people like Richard Owen and Gideon Mantell that we know something about the animals that were alive millions of years ago.

The all-important egg

It often takes a very long time to solve some scientific puzzles and many scientists may have to make discoveries before the answer becomes clear. One of these puzzles was to find out just how animals are born. In about 1750, Lazzaro Spallanzanni showed that sperm from a male animal had to enter a female before a baby animal could grow. However, that was not the end of the story.

Animal eggs?

In about 1674, when Anton van Leeuwenhoek looked at human sperm through a microscope, he thought that he saw tiny people. He believed that when the sperm entered a female these tiny people gradually grew until they were big enough to be born. An English doctor called William Harvey had another idea. He thought that all animals grow from an egg. The eggs of birds and fish were easy to see but no one had ever seen the egg of an animal like a cow or a human being, so Harvey could not be sure he was right.

Karl von Baer

Karl von Baer was a German scientist who was born in 1792. He, like Harvey, thought that animals must have eggs, so he began to search for the eggs of animals like cows, rabbits and dogs. These animals, that feed their babies with milk, are called **mammals**. Von Baer examined many different mammals and, in 1824, he finally found what he was looking for. He found a tiny, soft egg in the body of a female rabbit.

Karl von Baer (1792–1876). He discovered that mammals have eggs and studied the way babies grow from the egg. This was the start of the modern science of embryology.

This was not enough for von Baer and he continued his search. He soon found eggs inside a dog and, finally, he discovered the egg of a human being. This proved that mammals begin as eggs, even though they are born as living babies. Of course, mammal eggs are not like birds' eggs, they are very small and are not covered by a hard shell.

Changing eggs into animals

Von Baer went on to study the way a mammal egg grows into a small animal. He found that when the sperm from the

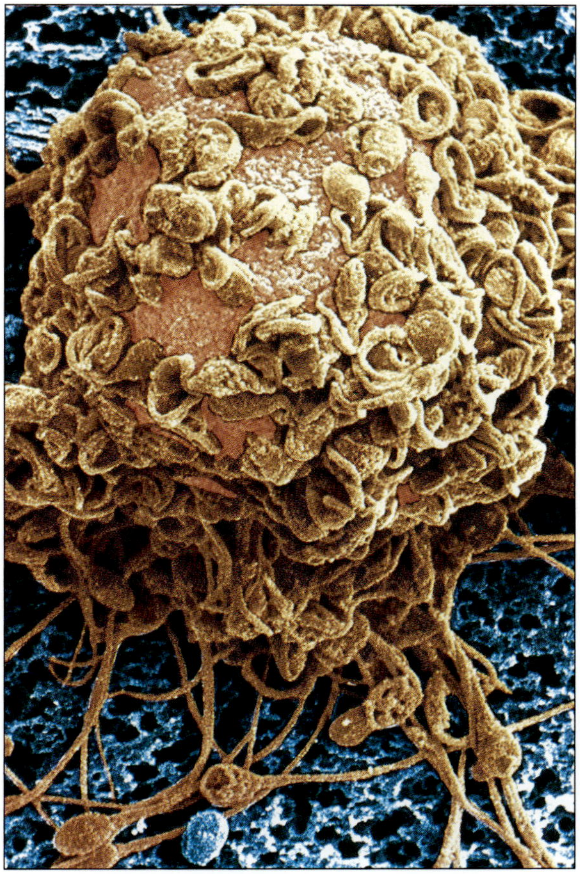

◀ **A human egg**. An electron microscope picture of a human egg enlarged about 1000 times. The egg (pale pink) is surrounded by tadpole-shaped sperm (pale brown). When a sperm enters the egg, a baby starts to develop.

▼ **Test tube baby**. Louise Brown was born in 1978. She was the first child to be born thanks to a new technique of fertilizing the mother's egg outside the body. The fertilized egg is placed inside the mother and the baby grows normally. These techniques are only possible because of Karl von Baer's discoveries.

male animal enters the the female animal it joins with one of the female's eggs. This egg then starts to grow into a new animal.

Von Baer once said 'If I could study an animal from its very beginning, if I could watch it from the very first instant the sperm enters the egg and study all the stages that it passes through until it becomes a complete adult, then I might understand how the animal's body is built; and this is one of the most extraordinary things in nature.' The study of the developing animal is called **embryology**. Today, embryology is one of the most important biological sciences and it started with Karl von Baer's determination to find a mammal's egg.

Scientists are now able to **fertilize** eggs outside the body and then replace the **embryo** into the mother so that it grows into a baby animal. This has helped people who could not have babies normally to have normal, healthy children.

The building blocks of life

All animals and plants are made up of small parts, called cells. Cells were first observed in 1665 by Robert Hooke, looking through an early microscope. He saw that cork, seen through a microscope, was like a collection of little boxes. He called these boxes cells, but he did not realize that cells are the building blocks of all living things.

Millions of cells

A German biologist called Theodor Schwann showed that all plants and animals are made up of cells. Schwann was born in 1810 and he studied medicine at the University of Berlin. There he began his most important work, studying animal **tissue** under the microscope. He found that all animal tissue was made up from small cells. Since he knew little about plants, Schwann asked Matthias Schleiden, who was a botanist, to study plants. Schleiden found that all plants were made up of cells, too. In 1839 Schwann and Schleiden decided that all living things are made up of cells.

By examining many different types of tissue with his microscope, Schwann found that there were many kinds of cells. The yolk of an ostrich egg is a single cell several centimetres across. Most cells, however, are only about a thousandth of a centimetre across. Some cells are round like balls, some are long and thin, some are shaped like tadpoles.

Theodor Schwann (1810–82), a German biologist who showed that all things are made up of cells. Some organisms, such as bacteria, have only one cell. A human body has a million million cells.

In the human body, there are a million million cells. There are blood cells, bone cells, nerve cells and others. Schwann also discovered that bacteria are made up of single cells.

How cells grow

By skilfully using his microscope, Schwann discovered that cells could grow and reproduce. This happens when one cell breaks or divides into two cells. Then these two cells divide to form four cells, and so on. This process is called **cell division** and it is the means by which plants and animals grow. For example, new cells form by cell division at the tip of a growing plant.

Schwann also studied the way animals grow from eggs. He discovered

▶ **Tomato cells**. This microscope photograph shows tomato cells, enlarged about 30 times. They are like bags of liquid. They form into rows to make plant tissue.

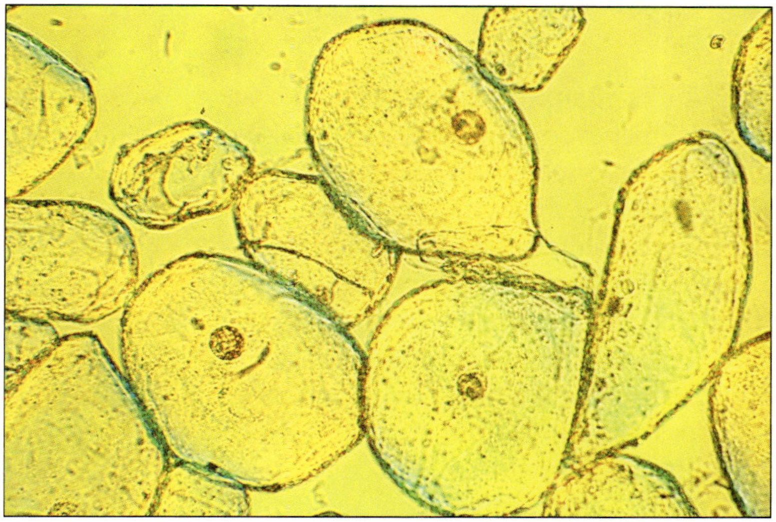

▼ **Cell division**. These microscope pictures show how a frog's egg divides as the tiny frog begins to grow. First there is one cell. This then divides into four cells, then eight cells, and so on, until there are enough cells to form the frog.

that the egg from which a baby animal grows is a single cell. He found that when sperm enters and fertilizes the egg, this single cell divides to form many cells. Some of the cells formed become bone, some become teeth, some become muscle, and so on. The process of division continues until there are enough cells to form the complete baby animal. Schwann was the first person to see this incredible development. His discovery was a major step in the study of **embryology**.

Charles Darwin

For many centuries, people believed that plants and animals never changed and would always be exactly as they were when they were created. Jean Lamarck, the famous scientist who invented the word 'biology', put forward a theory that, in fact, all living things gradually change to suit their circumstances. Unfortunately, his ideas were not quite accurate and it was Charles Darwin who discovered the way plants and animals have slowly changed over long periods of time. This is called **evolution**, which means 'slow unfolding'.

The voyage of the *Beagle*

Charles Darwin was born in Shrewsbury, in England, in 1809. He studied medicine but found that he could not bear to watch operations, which in those days were messy and painful. Also, he thought the medical lessons were boring. So he decided to become a clergyman and he went to Cambridge University to study religion. In his spare time, he liked to study insects and plants.

In 1831 Darwin was offered a job on a ship, the *Beagle*, that was just about to sail around the world. Darwin became the ship's naturalist. He was to study all the plants and animals found during the voyage. The voyage lasted five years.

On the voyage, the *Beagle* visited the Galapagos Islands, a group of twelve small islands in the Pacific Ocean. Darwin noticed that on each island there were many birds, called finches. He also noticed that on each island, the finches had different shaped beaks. Why was this? Darwin decided that it was because there was a different type of food on

The *Beagle* sailing along the coast of Tierra del Fuego, at the southernmost tip of America. The painting was done by the expedition's artist Conrad Martens. Darwin used the voyage of the *Beagle* to observe the great variety of life found in the Americas.

Darwin's notebooks kept during the voyage of the *Beagle* can be seen at the bottom right. The beautiful sketches show the different types of birds seen by Darwin during the trip. The magnolia flower (bottom right) is believed to resemble most closely the earliest flowering plants.

each island. Only birds that had a beak of the right shape could eat the food. The others died.

An unpopular theory

Darwin realized that the same process happened with all living things. At any one time, there were many different kinds of plants and animals alive but only those animals or plants that were suited to their surroundings survived. This is called 'survival of the fittest', or **natural selection**. Over millions of years, this process gradually changes plants and animals. They evolve until they are suited to their surroundings.

Making fun of Darwin. Many people thought that Darwin's ideas were ridiculous. Cartoons like this appeared in the newspapers. Because Darwin said that human beings were closely related to the apes, the cartoonist makes Darwin into an ape.

In 1859 Darwin put his ideas in a famous book called *The Origin of Species*. This caused many arguments because it seemed to disagree with what was written in the Bible. Another of his books, called *The Descent of Man*, caused even more trouble. In it, Darwin said that human beings were closely related to the apes. He thought that they had both evolved from a type of ape-man. For a time, the Church argued against his ideas because the Church taught that God had created people in the Garden of Eden.

Today, most people believe that Darwin was right. Evolution is one of the most important theories of modern science. It explains why there are so many different living things found in the world.

Gregor Mendel

Have you ever wondered why you have the same colour eyes as one of your parents or why you look like someone else in your family? It is because of **heredity**. Heredity is the way all living things pass on their characteristics to their descendants. The science of heredity was begun by Gregor Mendel.

Three generations: mother, daughter, granddaughter. How are they similar? Hair colour is one trait that is passed from one generation to the next according to the rules discovered by Gregor Mendel.

The gardening monk

Gregor Mendel was born in 1822 in the Austrian town of Heinzendorf. He was interested in science, particularly in botany, the study of plants. However, he became a monk and joined a remote monastery in Czechoslovakia. In the monastery, he had time to work in the garden and to do experiments with plants. He began to grow different types of sweet pea. Some of his sweet peas were tall plants and some were small or dwarf plants. Each year he would note the height of his plants, then he would put the fine powder, or **pollen**, found in the flowers of one plant onto the flowers of another. This is called crossing, or **cross pollinating**, one plant with another. When a plant has been pollinated it produces seeds. Mendel grew the seeds from his cross-pollinated plant to see if the new plant, called the **offspring**, was like its parents. He worked for eight years on his cross pollination experiments and during this time he planted over 10 000 sweet pea plants.

Gregor Mendel (1822–84) discovered that characteristcs are not passed from parents to their children by chance. There is a simple way of calculating which characteristics will be passed on. Gregor Mendel's ideas about heredity were ignored during his lifetime. Even Charles Darwin was too busy to read a letter from him that explained his ideas.

Family resemblances

Mendel found that crossing a tall plant with another tall plant produced tall plants. Crossing a dwarf plant with a dwarf plant gave dwarf plants. This was as he expected. However, crossing a tall plant with a dwarf plant gave him a surprise. The first year the plants he produced were all tall. He then divided these plants into two groups. He crossed a tall plant from one group with a tall plant from the other group. He found that the year after, a quarter of the plants produced were dwarf. What was causing tall plants to produce dwarf plants?

Mendel decided that the answer was that each parent plant gave either a 'tallness instruction' or a 'shortness instruction' to its offspring. A plant would be tall if it had a tallness instruction from a least one of its parents. Using this idea, Mendel was able to calculate the number of tall plants and short plants he could expect to grow. His experiments showed he was right. He was also able to calculate how many pink flowers he would get if he crossed white flowers with red flowers.

Mendel's laws in action. The parents of these chicks were a Rhode Island Red cockerel and a Light Sussex hen. The proportion of red to white chicks can be calculated using Mendel's laws of heredity.

A disappointing end

In 1865, Gregor Mendel proudly announced his findings to the local natural history society, but no one was very interested. Naturally, Gregor was disappointed. Then, in 1868, he was made chief monk of his monastery, so he had too little time for his experiments. It was only many years after his death that scientists realized how important his experiments had been. He had discovered that living things can pass on certain of their own characteristics to their offspring through a series of 'instructions'.

Doctor Morgan's fruit flies

Mendel's ideas about heredity were forgotten for many years. However, in about 1900, scientists began to be more interested in the subject. The scientist who revived Mendel's ideas was an American called Thomas Morgan.

Thomas Morgan was born in Kentucky in 1866. He studied biology at college and later he went to work at Johns Hopkins University in Maryland. In 1910 he began to experiment with fruit flies. Fruit flies are small insects that can be kept in bottles and fed on mashed banana. They have small, striped bodies, and usually have red eyes. The type of fruit fly Morgan used could produce offspring, or **breed**, very quickly, which made them ideal for studying the differences between parents and offspring.

Thomas Morgan (1866–1945). American biologist Thomas Morgan showed that Mendel's ideas about heredity were correct. He experimented with fruit flies and discovered how eye colour and wing shape were passed from parent fly to offspring.

The white-eyed fly

One day Morgan noticed that a male fly with white eyes had appeared in one of the bottles. Morgan was able to breed from this fly, producing normal, red-eyed flies. However, when he bred from these new red-eyed flies, some white-eyed offspring were also produced.

This reminded Morgan of Mendel's discoveries. Perhaps the 'instruction' for white eyes was being passed from parents to offspring, as Mendel had explained. Morgan did more experiments, breeding white-eyed males with red-eyed females. He used Mendel's ideas to work out how many of each type were to be expected among the offspring. There was just one complication. Only male flies were able to have white eyes. However, when Morgan had taken this into account, he found that Mendel's ideas correctly predicted how many of each type of fly he could expect.

Changing the instructions

Where did the 'instructions' Mendel had talked of come from? Morgan thought that they were small **particles** found in the cells of a plant or animal. He called

The experimental fly. The fruit fly is used in many genetic experiments because it breeds quickly. The fly on the right, with red eyes, is the natural or wild type. The fly on the left has different genes from the wild type, so it has different eye colour.

Genetics at work. The dog on the left is a Cavalier King Charles Spaniel. It has a normal nose. The dog on the right, a King Charles spaniel, has a squashed nose. Somehow its nose gene has been changed. People liked this nose and began to breed dogs to look like this. Morgan's experiments with fruit flies showed that once a gene's instructions have been changed it will pass on its new characteristics to its offspring.

these particles **genes**. In fruit flies, there is a gene that makes eyes red. There is another that makes eyes white. In peas, there is a tallness gene and a shortness gene. The genes are passed from parents to their offspring, and decide what the offspring will be like.

In Morgan's experiments, flies sometimes appeared with an unusual feature, such as a crumpled wing or no eyes. These features were always passed on to the offspring when the flies were bred. This showed that the gene for that feature had changed, and the new gene was passed to the offspring.

It was not until 1960, when scientists succeeded in separating a gene from its cell, that Morgan's theory about genes being particles was proved to be correct. The race was then on to find out how genes worked.

The first humans

In 1859 Charles Darwin was very unpopular with many people. His theory of evolution said that humans had developed from earlier ape-like creatures. This idea horrified religious people, but many scientists thought that Darwin was right. They began to search for the remains of these missing creatures. They were called the 'missing link' because they were thought to be half human and half ape and provided the link between the two species.

Neanderthal man. The fossil skull and bones of Neanderthal man were found in 1908 in a cave at La Chapelle-aux-Saints, France. The Neanderthals were a sturdy and successful race, short and thick set. Their body form was similar to modern people. They lived by hunting and gathering wild food, ranging across Europe about 130,000 to 35,000 years ago.

The oldest footprints in the world. Mary Leakey, a British scientist who has discovered many remains of early people, examines a trail of fossilized footprints found at Laetoli, Tanzania in 1978. The footprints were formed about 3.6 million years ago when one of our ancestors walked across a muddy stream bed and show that by this time our ancestors were walking upright.

In fact, the bones of an early human being had already been discovered. In 1856 a nearly complete skeleton had been found in a cave in Germany, but most of it had been thrown away. No one had realized what it was. A few years later, the remaining bones were examined more carefully. It was then realized that the bones belonged to a primitive type of human being. Most scientists thought these were the missing link between people and apes. The creatures were called **Neanderthal Man** because they were first found in the valley of Neanderthal, near Düsseldorf, in Germany.

The search for the missing link

In 1887 a young Dutch doctor called Eugène Dubois went to Indonesia to hunt for the missing link. Dubois thought that Neanderthal Man was not the missing link and he thought that the true missing link had probably lived in Asia.

Dubois went to the island of Sumatra in Indonesia. This island was the home of intelligent apes called orang-utans, so it seemed a good place to start. He found nothing in Sumatra, but he had more luck in Java, another Indonesian island.

In 1891 Dubois found a jaw bone, a tooth and part of the skull of a human-like creature. At first he thought they belonged to a chimpanzee, but later he found a leg bone as well. The leg bone was straight and obviously belonged to a creature that walked upright. The skull of the animal was large, showing that it was intelligent. Dubois called the creature **Java Man**, or **Homo Erectus**, upright man.

Homo Erectus lived about 1.5 million years ago. This is much earlier than Neanderthal Man, who lived about 50 000 years ago. Homo Erectus hunted large animals. These creatures were the first people to use fire to cook food and to keep warm.

The skull of Zinjanthropus found at Olduvai Gorge, Tanzania in 1959 by Mary Leakey. The background to the picture is the area of the excavation site. The skull is known as Zinj or 'Nutcracker Man' due to the size of its teeth. It is dated at 1.75 million years old and is thought to be a forebear of modern man. The skull was found near stone tools.

The Leakey family

Since then, the remains of even earlier people have been found. Important discoveries were made by Louis Leakey and his family at Olduvai Gorge, in East Africa. They found the remains of another type of early human being, called **Homo Habilis**. The name means 'handy man'. Homo Habilis lived about 2 million years ago. They used tools and probably walked upright. They were also probably the first true people, although scientists are still not completely certain about this. It is always possible that someone will discover an even earlier skeleton.

The insect man

Many people do not like insects. They are frightened of them and call them 'creepy crawlies'. One man, however, was fascinated by insects and he wrote many books about their lives and how they behave. His name was Jean Fabre and he was a French scientist. One of his books was called *The Life of the Fly*, and another was called *The Life of the Weevil.* They were very interesting and clear to read and they were enjoyed by thousands of children in France. However, Fabre was almost unknown outside France and it was not until he was old that people realized that his work was important.

Frenchman Jean Fabre (1823–1915) was noted for his vivid descriptions of the life of wasps, bees and other insects. No detail of an insect's life was too small or unimportant for him. His books describing insect life became bestsellers.

A lonely life

Jean Fabre was born in 1823 in the town of Saint-Léons in Aveyron, in France. He was very poor almost all his life but, despite his poverty, he managed to study at the local university. When his studies were over he became a teacher in Avignon in the South of France, where he taught the local children for 20 years.

Fabre retired from teaching in 1871 and devoted the rest of his life to studying insects. He lived a lonely life in the country. He was always in the fields watching how insects behaved and lived. He was too poor to travel, so the insects he studied were those that he found in the districts around his home. He was particularly interested in the spider, fly, bee, grasshopper and wasp.

Are insects intelligent?

Fabre was the first to discover how wasps paralyse their **prey** by injecting a poison that makes the victim unable to move. The prey is kept, alive but unable to move, in the wasp nest as food for the young wasps. Fabre was puzzled by this behaviour. How could wasps know how to do this?

He decided that insects were intelligent and that they learn to paralyse their prey by watching other wasps. This

◀ **Guided by instinct**. Fabre studied how wasps, such as this digger wasp, paralyse their prey. He thought that this showed that the wasps were intelligent. But fabre was wrong. Instinct is guiding the wasp, not intelligence.

▼ **Guided by scent.** Many moths, like this Chinese Oak Silkmoth, have large feathery antennae. Fabre discovered that they use the antennae to detect faint smells which guide the moths to their mates.

idea was wrong. We know now that insects have a natural tendency to behave in certain ways. When they are born they already know how to get food and survive. Wasps are born knowing exactly how to sting their prey to paralyse it. This tendency to behave in a certain way is called **instinct**.

Perfuming the air

Fabre also observed that some male moths could smell a female moth several kilometres away and fly straight towards her. Other naturalists found this hard to believe, but Fabre was right. The female moth gives out a powerful smelling chemical that makes the male moth fly in the right direction. This helps moths find each other at breeding time. This discovery is very important for anyone trying to control some insect pests because they can trick insects with false chemical smells and stop them breeding.

It was not until he was nearly 80 years old that Fabre became famous for his discoveries about insects. He was honoured by the French government and was given a small salary to live on. Fabre died in 1915. His discoveries about how and why insects behave as they do has helped people control harmful insects and make use of beneficial ones.

Animal behaviour

Ordinary people have always enjoyed watching animals but it is only recently that scientists have studied how animals behave. Among the first scientists to study this subject were two Austrians called Konrad Lorenz and Karl von Frisch. They were awarded the Nobel Prize in 1973 for their discoveries.

Mother Goose?

Konrad Lorenz was born in 1903 in Vienna, the capital of Austria. When he was young he lived in a huge house near the Danube river. The house was large enough for many pets and Konrad kept ducklings, fish and dogs. He even had a flock of jackdaws in the attic of the

▲ **German zoologist, Karl von Frisch (1866–1982)**, who began with Konrad Lorenz the scientific study of animal behaviour. He discovered how bees communicate with each other by 'dances' within the hive.

◀ **Konrad Lorenz (1903–1989) and his 'family'**. Lorenz was one of the first scientists to study how animals behave. Later he used his discoveries to explain how humans behave.

house. He watched how they behaved and kept records of their behaviour. This was the beginning of a life-long interest. Konrad's father was a famous doctor and he wanted Konrad to become a doctor too, but Konrad had other ideas. He was interested in animals, not human beings, so he became a **zoologist** at the university in Vienna.

At university Lorenz studied the way birds learn to recognize their mothers. He found that some birds think that the first thing they see after hatching is their mother. To prove this, Lorenz raised some geese. He was the first creature they saw when they were hatched so they thought he was their mother! The young geese followed him everywhere he went. In another experiment, he persuaded a jackdaw to think it was a crow. It spent its time flying around with a flock of crows. These experiments showed that animal behaviour is more complicated than many people had expected.

Dancing bees

Karl von Frisch was also born in Vienna, in 1886. Like Lorenz, he studied the way animals behave. He found that fish have good hearing and can recognize different colours. However, he is most famous for his discoveries about bees.

Karl von Frisch found that bees could recognize different smells and tastes. He also found that bees do a special dance when they return to the hive with nectar, the sweet liquid they collect from flowers that they use to make honey. This dance tells the other bees where to find the nectar. There are two kinds of dance, a 'round' dance and a 'tail-waggling' dance. The round dance means that the nectar is near the hive. The tail-waggling dance means that the nectar is further away. The speed of the waggle tells the other bees the distance to the nectar. The direction of the dance shows the direction to the nectar, using the Sun as a guide. Once they have seen the dance, other bees can then find their way to the nectar. von Frisch's discoveries showed that insects can communicate with each other, even though they cannot speak.

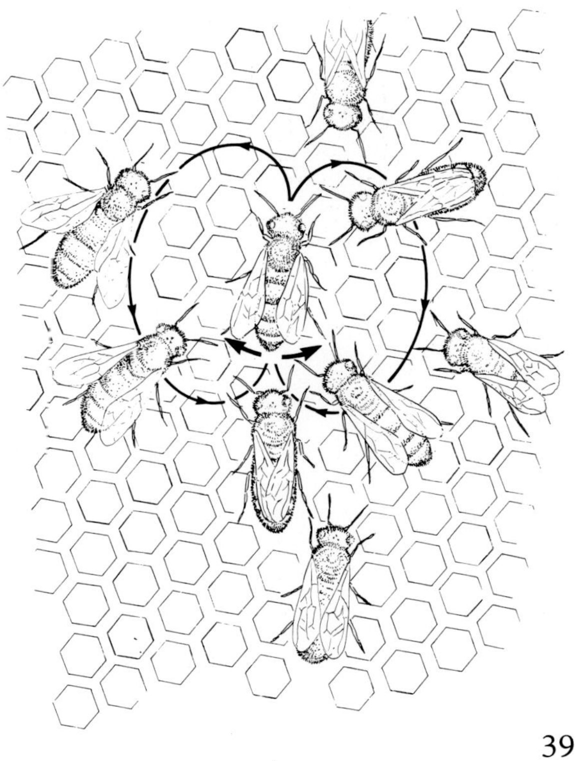

The bees' dance. When a bee returns to the hive with nectar it dances to communicate to the other bees where to find the nectar. The rapid, complicated movements indicate the distance and direction of the nectar.

How do genes work?

Thomas Morgan discovered the gene in 1910 but he did not know exactly what a gene was. All he knew was that genes decide how closely children resemble their parents. Many scientists asked 'What is a gene?', and 'How do genes work?' These were important questions. If scientists knew the answers, they might be able to cure certain types of disease and produce better crops and feed more people. It took a long time to find the answers. The first step was taken when scientists started to use bacteria to study genes.

Fast-breeding cells

Bacteria are small, single-celled creatures that can only be seen under a microscope. Some bacteria are harmful and cause diseases like typhoid fever. Other bacteria are helpful. They help rot dead plants and animals. There are even some useful bacteria that help natural processes like turning milk into cheese.

Bacteria are used in experiments to discover how genes work because they breed quickly. Some can produce offspring in about 20 minutes! This means that scientists who use genes from bacteria do not have to wait a long time to see if offspring resemble their parents.

A mysterious substance

In 1944 three American scientists were using bacteria in their experiments. They were Oswald Avery, Colin MacLeod and Maclyn McCarty. Although they were using a harmless bacteria they found that these bacteria could be changed into a dangerous type. This happened when a

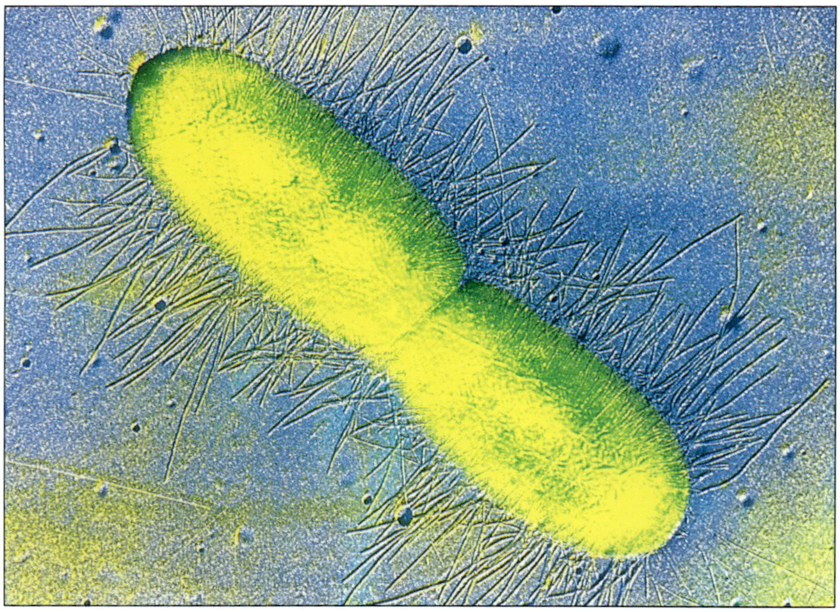

A useful bacterium. This electron microscope photograph shows the bacterium called *Escherichia coli*, magnified about 20 000 times. This bacteria normally lives harmlessly in the human intestine but it is used in experiments to study how genes work. The bacteria shown is just starting to divide into two by splitting in the middle.

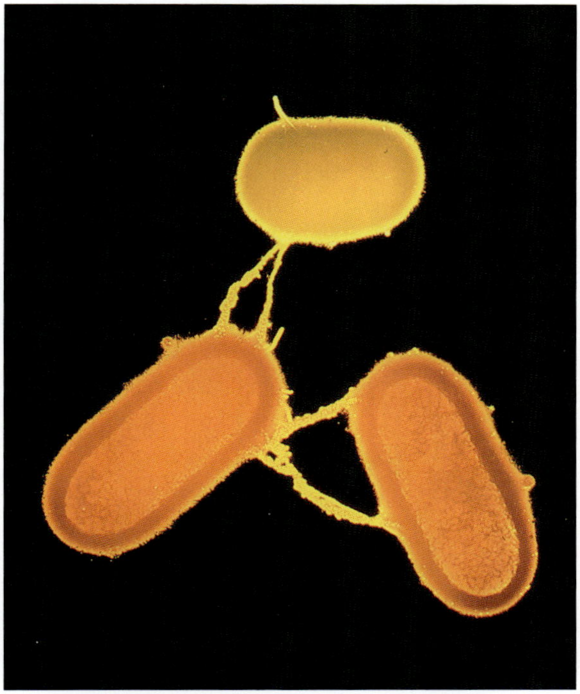

Exchanging DNA. These *Escherichia coli* bacteria are exchanging DNA using the thin tubes connecting them together. This exchange of DNA can convert the bacteria from the normal harmless type that live in our intestines to a type that causes infections. The photograph is magnified about 8000 times.

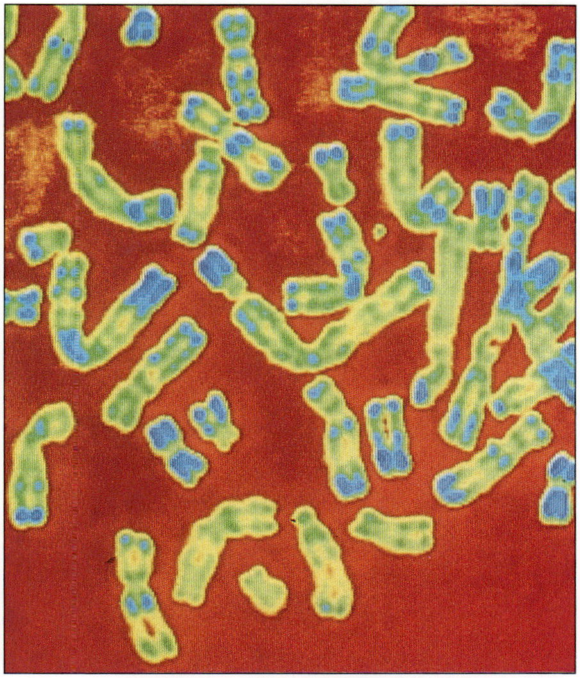

Packets of DNA. In all but the simplest living things, the DNA is contained in small bundles called **chromosomes**. Human cells have 45 chromosomes, like those shown in the electron microscope photograph.

substance called deoxyribonucleic acid was injected into the bacteria. Scientists call this substance **DNA** for short. The three scientists found that DNA could change one type of bacteria into another type and when the new bacteria was bred its offspring were dangerous, too. This meant that the DNA had changed the genes in the bacteria.

DNA was surprising in other ways, too. Alfred Hershey and Martha Chase, two American biologists, found that DNA could make copies of itself and that the amount of DNA in a bacteria could increase. This is not the same as breeding because only living things—breed, and DNA is not living.

Gradually, scientists decided that genes must be made of DNA. When plants or animals reproduce, DNA from the parents must pass to the offspring. This DNA must carry a message that tells the offspring how it should grow. Scientists did not know exactly how DNA was able to do this, and they did not know how DNA was able to reproduce itself. However, they had made the all-important first discovery that such a substance existed. The mystery of just how DNA works was solved in 1953 by scientists at Cambridge university in England.

The DNA story

In 1951 a young American scientist called James Watson travelled to Cambridge University, in England. He was determined to find out how genes worked. At Cambridge, Watson teamed up with Francis Crick, an English scientist who was also interested in genes. They knew that genes were made of DNA and they decided to discover how DNA was made up.

They also knew that all substances are made up of tiny particles called **molecules**. Molecules are groups of even smaller particles, called **atoms**, joined together. Watson and Crick wanted to know how the atoms were arranged in a DNA molecule.

James Watson (left) and Francis Crick (right) with their model of the DNA molecule. In 1962 they, together with Maurice Wilkins, were awarded the Nobel Prize for discovering how DNA was made up. This was one of the most important discoveries ever.

Unravelling the mystery

Other scientists at this time were using **X-rays** to find out how atoms were joined together to make molecules. X-rays are powerful bursts of energy that can pass straight through many substances. When a narrow beam of X-rays is shone onto a substance some of the X-rays are reflected, or bounced off. The scientists measured the angles of the reflections and from these measurements they were able to calculate how the atoms of the substance were joined together.

Watson and Crick found a third person to help in their research. He was Maurice Wilkins, who worked at London University. He had been studying DNA using X-rays for some time. He thought that the atoms in DNA were probably arranged in a sort of spiral, or corkscrew, shape, but he could not puzzle out exactly how the atoms were organized.

A spiral staircase

Watson and Crick decided to try to build a model of the DNA molecule. They used small balls to show where the atoms were and joined the balls together with bits of wire to form a model of the molecule.

At last, they found the solution. The atoms in DNA were joined together in a

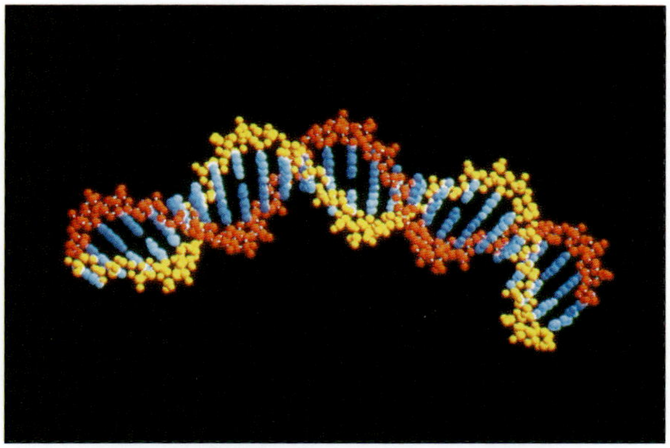

A computer drawing of the DNA molecule. The molecule consists of two strands wrapped around each other. The sequence of atoms along the strands forms a 'code' or message which is carried from parents to their offspring. This ensures that parents and offspring are similar.

spiral shape. There were, in fact, two spirals of atoms twisting around each other and the spirals were joined in the middle. The whole molecule looked like a spiral staircase.

They saw that the atoms forming the steps of the spiral staircase were arranged in a particular way. The atoms formed a type of code and this code told a new cell how it was to grow. This was how the DNA in genes made sure that offspring resembled their parents. At last, the puzzle was solved.

Changing the code of life

In 1962 Watson, Crick and Wilkins were awarded the Nobel Prize for their important discovery. Since then, other scientists have learned how to alter the DNA code. This is called **genetic engineering**. Genetic engineering has led to many benefits. Scientists have developed new cures for diseases that are caused by faulty DNA. They have found ways to make cheap medicines from bacteria that have had their genes altered. They are able to improve the genes of farm animals so that food is produced more efficiently.

Research on human DNA, using a computer-controlled system for reading the coded sequence in the human DNA molecule. The pattern of bands seen bottom left reveals part of the human genetic code. This type of research has brought cures for some diseases caused by faulty DNA, and has led to improved medicines and treatment of diseases.

Time chart

Date	Pioneer	Achievement
336BC	Aristotle	Begins writing his encyclopedia of all knowledge
1590	Zacharias Janssen	Makes the first microscope
1665	Robert Hooke	Discovers the cell, using a microscope
1669	Jan Swammerdam	Discovers that a bee's eye is made up of many eyes
1674	Anton van Leeuwenhoek	Observes bacteria with a simple hand-held microscope
1716	Stephen Hales	Studies the circulation of sap in plants
1750	Lazzaro Spallanzani	Studies how life begins
1758	Carl von Linné (Linnaeus)	Develops the modern system of naming animals and plants
1801	Jean Lamarck	Suggests that animals evolve over long periods of time
1822	William Beaumont	Studies how we digest our food with the help of a soldier who has a hole in his stomach
1822	Gideon Mantell	Discovers the bones of a dinosaur called the iguanodon
1824	Karl von Baer	Discovers the egg of a mammal
1839	Theodor Schwann	Describes animal and plant cells in detail
1858	Charles Darwin	Announces the theory of evolution by natural selection
1859	Charles Darwin	Publishes *The Origin of Species*
1865	Gregor Mendel	Discovers the way characteristics are carried from parents to children
1871	Jean Fabre	Studies the life of insects
1891	Eugène Dubois	Discovers the bones of an early human being

Date	Pioneer	Achievement
1910	Thomas Morgan	Proves Mendel's ideas are correct
1930	Konrad Lorenz	Studies how animals learn
1944	Oswald Avery, Colin MacLeod and Maclyn McCarty	Prove that genes are made of DNA
1953	Francis Crick, James Watson and Maurice Wilkins	Discover the structure of DNA and how it carries the information that determines the characteristics of offspring

Glossary

acid: a substance that can dissolve other substances. Acids in the stomach dissolve food

artery: a blood vessel or tube that carries blood from the heart to the other parts of the body

artificial insemination: taking sperm from a male animal and putting it into a female animal so that she produces a baby

atom: a very small particle

bacteria: a tiny single-celled creature

biology: the study of living things

biologist: a scientist who studies living things

botany: the study of plants

breed: to produce offspring

cell: the smallest piece of a living plant or animal

cell division: the way in which an animal or plant cell breaks, or divides, into two cells

chemist: a person who studies chemistry

chemistry: the science that studies what substances are made of, how they react together, and what properties they have

circulation: the way a liquid such as blood or sap moves round inside a living thing

classify: to group together plants, animals or other objects that are similar

corpuscle: a blood cell

cross pollinating: putting the pollen from one plant on the flowers of another plant of the same kind so that seeds are produced

digest: to soften food in the stomach so it can be used by the body

dinosaur: a giant lizard that lived millions of years ago

DNA: short for deoxyribonucleic acid, a substance that forms the genes in living cells

embryo: a young animal before it is born

embryology: the study of how embryos grow

evolution: the way in which plants and animals have changed gradually over millions of years

evolve: to change gradually

experiment: a test carried out in controlled conditions to discover something new or to prove that an idea is correct

female: an animal who can lay eggs or have babies

fertilize: to make something grow. Sperm fertilizes an egg

fossil: the hardened remains of a long-dead animal or plant usually found in rocks

gene: a small particle inside an animal or plant cell that decides what the offspring of the cell will be like

genetic engineering: ways of changing genes to produce new types of animals and plants

genus: a group of plants or animals that are similar

heredity: the way young animals and plants have similar characteristics to their parents

Homo Erectus: a type of ape-like human that lived long ago, and walked in an erect or upright position. Also called Java Man

Homo Habilis: a type of ape-like human that lived long ago and made simple tools. Probably the first true human being

iguana: a type of lizard found in South America

iguanodon: a very large dinosaur that looked like a iguana

image: the picture formed by light passing through a lens

instinct: a way of behaving that an animal is born with

intestine: the tube that passes downwards out of the stomach. It carries digested food

invertebrate: an animal that has no backbone

lens: a piece of glass or clear material that has curved sides

male: an animal that produces sperm but cannot have babies or lay eggs

mammal: a hairy animal that produces milk to feed its young

microscope: a magnifying instrument used to see very small things

molecule: a tiny particle that is made up of atoms

natural selection: a gradual process in evolution in which only plants or animals that are suited to their surroundings survive

Neanderthal Man: a type of ape-like human who lived long ago in Europe

Nobel Prize: a prize given each year to someone who has done important work or who has made an important scientific discovery

offspring: the young produced by a plant or animal

particle: a very small piece of material

pasteurization: a process used to make food stay fresh by heating it until all germs are killed

physics: the science that studies matter, the forces of nature and the different forms of energy, such as heat, light and motion

physicist: a person who studies physics

pollen: the tiny yellow grains produced by flowers that eventually help produce seeds

prey: an animal that is hunted by another animal for food

sap: the liquid inside a plant

science: the study of the way the world works by using experiments and careful observation

species: varieties of animals or plants that are very similar

sperm: the liquid produced by male animals that can cause a female to have a baby

theory: an idea that explains why something happens

tissue: material from a living plant or animal

vein: a blood vessel or tube that carries blood from the body to the heart

vertebrate: an animal with a backbone

X-ray: a beam, or ray, that can pass through solid things

zoology: the study of animals

zoologist: a scientist who studies animals

Index